INTRODUCTION

The Scholastic *Writing Guides* series provides teachers with ideas and projects that promote a range of writing, bringing insights from educational research into the classroom. Each guide explores a different type of writing and provides example material, background information, photocopiable activities and teaching suggestions. Their aim is to enable teachers to guide the writing process, share planning ideas and develop themes as a context for writing activities.

The materials:
● motivate children with interesting activities
● break complex types of writing into manageable teaching units
● focus on and develop the typical features of particular types of writing
● provide original approaches to teaching.

Each book is divided into sections, beginning with examples of the type of writing being taught. These are followed by ideas for developing writing and projects that will extend over a series of sessions.

SECTION ONE: USING GOOD EXAMPLES

Section One looks at good examples of the genre, with the emphasis on using texts to stimulate and develop writing. Two example texts are shared, and questions that focus the discussion on their significant features are suggested. This is followed by activities that explore what the texts can teach us about writing, enabling teachers to compare the two texts and to go on to model the type of writing presented in the guide.

SECTION TWO: DEVELOPING WRITING

Section Two moves from reading to writing. This section provides activities that prompt and support children in planning and writing. A range of approaches includes planning templates and strategies to stimulate ideas. The activities refine children's ideas about the type of writing being developed and give them focused writing practice in the context of scaffolded tasks. Teacher's notes support each activity by explaining the objective and giving guidance on delivery.

SECTION THREE: WRITING

Section Three moves on to writing projects. Building upon the earlier work in Section Two, these projects aim to develop the quality of writing and provide a selection of ideas for class or group work on a particular theme or idea. The teacher may choose to use some or all of the ideas presented in each project as a way of weaving the strategies developed in Section Two into a more complex and extended writing task.

SECTION FOUR: REVIEW

Section Four supports the assessment process. Children are encouraged to reflect on the type of writing they are tackling and to evaluate how effectively their work has met the criteria for the genre identified in Section One.

Read all about it!

Note-able discovery

A GIRL'S message in a bottle was picked up 600 miles away by the Swedish cousin of her school classmate.

Kaylee Richards' note was found on a beach by Camilla Larsson, 13, two years after it was sent.

But now Kaylee, 11, and Camilla – who began writing to each other – have discovered a mutual acquaintance.

A letter from Camilla said she had two cousins, Amelia and Christopher, who lived in England.

Kaylee sat next to a girl in primary school called Amelia – and remembered her brother was Christopher.

She told Camilla and heard back: "Amelia IS my cousin and she has told me all about you."

Kaylee, from Longbenton, Newcastle-upon-Tyne, said: "Now I'd love it if we could all get together."

Her father Michael, 46, added: "This must be a million-to-one chance, an incredible coincidence."

The Mirror, 4th October 1999

These are the headlines

Dogs are left £30m

AN aristocrat has left his £30million fortune to his only friends – his dogs.

The Mirror, 6th June 1998

FLAMING DAY OFF

A FIREMAN who has never tackled a blaze in 29 years missed out when flames finally flared – on his day off.

The Mirror, 24th November 1999

Yes... peas in our time

By AIDAN McGURRAN

PEAS are to stay on a restaurant chain's menu by popular demand.

The Mirror, 6th June 2001

DOG SURVIVES 140FT PLUNGE

By RICHARD WHITE

HENRY the retriever escaped with just an injured paw after plunging 140ft from a cliff top.

The Mirror, 3rd October 2001

SECTION ONE

USING GOOD EXAMPLES

Children learn to write from reading: everything they read helps them to develop the structure of their own writing. This is especially true when it comes to news writing – an area that benefits from observing experts deploy the tricks of the trade. In this section, children will look at the features of a news story, focusing in particular on headlines and opening lines before moving to a comparison of texts.

In an area like news, where texts date quickly, it is vital that the children bring their learning to bear on fresh, new stories. Encourage them to read newspapers at home, cut out interesting stories and bring them in to school, sticking them on a chart, in a folder or a scrapbook.

Shared activities

Read all about it!

This piece from *The Mirror* presents a model of news reporting. Display the article on photocopiable page 4 and read it through with the children. Ask them what they notice that is different to normal writing, including:

● **Headline:** a short, snappy line that indicates the content of the story and attracts the reader. (These are looked at more closely in the next activity.)

● **Opening paragraph:** this gives the basic information about the story – who, what, where and when – summing it up in a sentence or two. Point out that even if we only read this first paragraph we would have the basic facts of the whole story. Given that news stories are often cut from the end in order to fit the space available, and that readers often read only the first part of a news story, this is a common feature of a news recount.

● **Details:** the rest of the story gives progressively more information about the events and those who were involved.

● **Quotes:** these are used to give an insight into how those involved felt about the events of the story. They provide an outlet for opinions and different thoughts the participants might express. Whereas journalists recount stories as objectively as possible, giving just the facts, a quote gives an insight into how a participant of a story has been affected.

In addition to these features, there is the overarching fact that the story must be of interest. Ask the children to look at the extract to see what it is about stories like these that grab our attention. The rarity of an event, human interest – a story we can relate to and empathise with – and an interesting outcome all add to the make-up of a good news story.

These are the headlines

The selection of headlines and opening sentences on photocopiable page 5 helps the children to focus on the very start of a newspaper story, with a selection of opening paragraphs given as examples.

Ask the children what headlines tell us about a news story. Show them just the headlines from photocopiable page 5, with each of the first paragraphs covered up, and ask them to guess what each story is about. Make a list of the children's suggestions, then reveal the opening sentences and ask the children to check how well they guessed.

Talk about word play in some of the headlines ('Flaming day off' and 'Yes... peas in our time'). Can anybody explain the pun in 'Flaming day off'? or the reference to 'Peace in our time'? (The children may need support in working out these references.) Are the headlines are funny? Would any of the headlines make them want to read more? The class could vote on the headline they would most like to explore further.

Point out that some of the stories have a byline before the main story starts. This tells us the name of the reporter who has written the story, and is often seen when a famous journalist has written the story.

Now look at the opening paragraphs, and recap on how the complete story is summarised in the opening paragraph. Talk about how the rest of the story is elaboration of detail, comment and quotation.

Missing words

Make copies of photocopiable page 5 with the words *Dogs*, *Flaming*, *Survives* and *Peas* blacked out. Ask the children to show these headlines to adults at home and school, and to record suggestions of the missing words. Gather the children's ideas together and compare suggestions. Did anybody correctly guess any of the words? What were the most common suggestions? Who correctly identified the 'Yes... peas in our time' reference?

Annotated news

Photocopiable page 8 gives the children an opportunity to look at the 'Note-able discovery' story in more detail by focusing on the specific features of a news story that they identified earlier. Read through the story again, and invite children to offer their views on the four questions. The same four questions could easily be applied to any other news story the children may have read, and each of these areas is developed further in Section Two.

Alternative headlines

Using the headlines on photocopiable page 9 (and any of the children's own ideas), ask small 'editorial teams' to cut out and sort the headlines to match each of the stories on page 5, then to select their favourite, discussing which they would use if they were editing a real newspaper. Point out the need for relevance to the story and interesting or entertaining wording in a headline.

Taking ideas further

Comparing news

Using 'Note-able discovery' from page 4, two of the stories from photocopiable page 5, and one they have collected from home or school, ask the children to complete their own copy of the grid on photocopiable page 10, which will help them to identify common features in the four stories. As they are completing the sheet, encourage the children to consider how well each story fulfils the criteria shown. Which has the most striking headline? Which most effectively answers the questions and gives an idea as to the story's content?

In the news

The poster on photocopiable page 11 draws together the ideas the children have looked at in Section One. Display this poster where the children can see it as they develop their ideas over the rest of the activities.

Annotated news

Headline

How does the headline use words in a clever way?

_____

_____

_____

First paragraph

What questions are answered in this paragraph?

_____

_____

_____

_____

Details

How many details can you find in this story?

_____

_____

_____

_____

Note-able discovery

A GIRL'S message in a bottle was picked up 600 miles away by the Swedish cousin of her school classmate.

Kaylee Richards' note was found on a beach by Camilla Larsson, 13, two years after it was sent.

But now Kaylee, 11, and Camilla – who began writing to each other – have discovered a mutual acquaintance.

A letter from Camilla said she had two cousins, Amelia and Christopher, who lived in England.

Kaylee sat next to a girl in primary school called Amelia – and remembered her brother was Christopher.

She told Camilla and heard back: "Amelia IS my cousin and she has told me all about you."

Kaylee, from Longbenton, Newcastle-upon-Tyne, said: "Now I'd love it if we could all get together."

Her father Michael, 46, added: "This must be a million-to-one chance, an incredible coincidence."

The Mirror, 4th October 1999

Quotes

Who is quoted and how do they feature in the story?

_____

_____

_____

Alternative headlines

DOG SURVIVES

Hot Dogs

WHAT THE BLAZES?

Bark to Bank

PEAS-FUL MENU

Fireman has problems

RESTAURANT CHANGES MENU

LUCKY DOGS

You're Fired

FIRE! FIRE!

Flying Dog

Rich Dogs

Pea-Po!

DOG DIVING

BARKING MAD

Peas are back

UNFROZEN PEAS

WOOF WOOF MILLIONAIRES

Day off, off

30 MILLION DOGS

Comparing news

Choose four different news stories. Number them 1 to 4 and answer these questions for each story.

The two most striking words in the headline	Question(s) answered in the first sentence	What the story might be about	What works well in the first part

In the news

Think why the story will interest readers

**Answer the questions:
Who? What? When? Where? Why?**

**Give the story a snappy
and striking headline**

Make sure you pack in all the details

**Use quotes from people,
showing what they saw and thought**

Don't use too many words

Make the story interesting

SECTION TWO

DEVELOPING WRITING

Here, the features of a news story that the children identified in Section One form the basis for further work on building skills in writing news stories.

As you work through this section, there are some vital ongoing resources you will need in your classroom. The first is a steady supply of real newspapers: if you can, order a daily paper if your class doesn't already receive one. Mix styles of newspaper: broadsheet and tabloid; local and national. A steady stream of other news is also useful. This could involve listening to radio bulletins or watching television lunchtime news. There should be space on the classroom wall for children to put stories that might merit following up. Stress that if a story is worth telling between two people, there's a good chance others would be interested in it. Things happening in the school or community will provide worthwhile material, as will holidays, visits, meetings of the Governors – all are possible starting points.

When making notes, it adds excitement if children can use reporter's notepads. ICT is also a vital tool and should be used wherever possible.

MORNING CONFERENCE

OBJECTIVE

■ To devise questions for use in news-gathering.

WHAT YOU NEED

Newspaper stories, paper, writing materials.

WHAT TO DO

Ask the children, in groups of four or more, to hold a 'morning conference' as if they were working on a newspaper. Explain that in these meetings stories are discussed, deciding what needs to be found out as part of the reporting process.

Tell the children to note down questions around four stories (school and community news, or from a national newspaper). They should write a one-sentence summary of each story, then, as a group, think of four things they would need to find out about each news item. If, for example, the school's heating has broken down, they could ask *How will the children keep warm?*, *What caused it to break down?* or *When will it be repaired?* As was noted in Section One, good news stories must be of interest to the reader. Ask the children to think what a reader might ask when making their notes.

FIRST SENTENCE

OBJECTIVE

■ To structure the information given in the opening sentence of a news story.

WHAT YOU NEED

Photocopiable page 17, newspaper stories, writing materials.

WHAT TO DO

The secret of a good news story is to answer six key questions in the first paragraph. Four of these should explain the *Who? What? When?* and *Where?* of the story, and should be covered in the opening sentence. (Who is involved? What happened? and so on.) The other two questions – *How?* and *Why?* – can be explained later.

Ask the children to consider the following example:

> *The School Caretaker (who) said yesterday (when) that the School Hall (where) would be colder than usual (what) because the heating has broken down (why).*

Point out that this extract answers five of the six key questions in the opening sentence and means that, if necessary, the rest of the story can be cut (as often happens in a real newspaper where space is short) and it will still make sense.

Ask the children to choose up to three news stories from the class collection and to work individually on photocopiable page 17, answering the key questions for each. Using this information, ask the children to create an opening sentence for each story that answers three or four (or more) of these key questions.

WHY AND HOW
WHAT YOU NEED
Completed photocopiable page 17, newspaper stories, small pieces of card, paper, writing materials.

WHAT TO DO
Recap on the previous activity, and how the children tried to answer four of the six key questions in their opening sentences. Ask them to write one of the opening sentences on a small piece of card, and to think now about answering the remaining two questions: *How?* and *Why?*

If, for example, children have written an opening sentence *Laura caught a train yesterday*, they will need to expand this sentence to include more information. They may want to consider questions like: how an event occurred; how someone managed to do something; why these events took place; and why they matter.

Answers to *How?* and *Why?* questions can be written on further pieces of card and placed around the original sentence. These can then be sorted to identify two or three that could be incorporated into the news story.

This may produce: *Laura went to the station and caught a train. She was going to her Aunt's birthday party and bought a ticket using all the money she had saved*, which now also covers the why and how of the story.

OBJECTIVE
■ To develop the construction of recount sentences in a news story.

WHAT DID THEY SAY?
WHAT YOU NEED
Photocopiable page 18 (one copy per pair of children and one enlarged copy), blank paper, writing materials.

OBJECTIVE
■ To explore the use of quotes in a news story.

WHAT TO DO
Look at the scene on page 18 together. Talk about what you can see, and ask the children to think about the story that is unfolding. Can they suggest who the different participants are, what is happening, and how they might be reacting?

In pairs, ask the children to try to think what each character may be saying, and to fill in the speech bubbles on the sheet accordingly. Ask them to think how these speech bubbles might later be incorporated into a news story.

On another sheet of paper, ask the children to try to put these quotes into sentences, punctuated with speech marks, as they would appear in a news report (for example, *Ms Parks the zookeeper said 'I tried to remain calm, but...'*). As the children finish, share some of their ideas.

IT'S A FACT
WHAT YOU NEED
Photocopiable page 19, scissors, board or flip chart.

OBJECTIVE
■ To distinguish between fact and opinion.

WHAT TO DO
Split the board into two columns headed *Fact* and *Opinion*. Make some statements

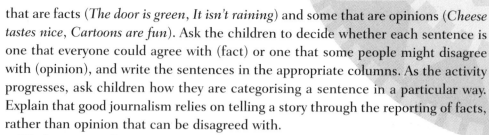

that are facts (*The door is green, It isn't raining*) and some that are opinions (*Cheese tastes nice, Cartoons are fun*). Ask the children to decide whether each sentence is one that everyone could agree with (fact) or one that some people might disagree with (opinion), and write the sentences in the appropriate columns. As the activity progresses, ask children how they are categorising a sentence in a particular way. Explain that good journalism relies on telling a story through the reporting of facts, rather than opinion that can be disagreed with.

Working in small groups on a copy of photocopiable page 19, ask the children to cut out the statements and sort them into two piles – fact and opinion. Once they have finished, bring the whole class together to see if they have all ended up with similarly sorted piles. How did they know which were fact and which were opinion?

QUESTION GENERATOR
WHAT YOU NEED
Photocopiable page 20, board or flip chart.

WHAT TO DO
Brainstorm some news stories that the children have seen on television or in newspapers recently. Choose one story, and together think of questions you could ask about the event, either of the people involved or about the story in general. List the first word or words of each question on the board, for example *When was..? Why did..? What made you..?* Point out some of the question words that are commonly appearing. You could look back at the children's work from 'Morning conference' and 'First sentence' (page 12) to provide a basis for this activity.

Working individually, ask the children to think of questions surrounding a particular news story – either in the news or from the local community. Explain that they should write eight questions they could ask if they were investigating the story, based on the sentence starters on the board and around the page. Challenge the children to use a different sentence starter for each question.

OBJECTIVE
■ To devise a wider range of investigative questions.

NEWS NOTES
WHAT YOU NEED
A news story copied on to acetate (this should be done in accordance with your school's NLA licence), OHP, notepads, writing materials, board or flip chart.

OBJECTIVE
■ To develop skills of note-making.

WHAT TO DO
Tell the children that you are going to read a news story to them, and that they should make notes on what you tell them. Explain that they need not write whole sentences, just key words that will help them recall the information.

Read through the news story at average speed, judging the pace by how quickly the children are taking notes, but always ahead of the writing.

After you have read the story once, share what the children recorded. Write the key points they can recall on the board then display the story on the OHP. What facts or quotes did they manage to record? Were any left out or noted inaccurately?

To help the children understand the skills of note-making, look at the difference between content words and function words. A sentence like: *A robber ran into the bank and stole all the pencils* contains certain words (*robber, bank, stole, pencils*) that refer to things or actions – these are content words. Function words (*A, into, the*) link the content together, providing structure and communicating the content. In note-taking, the reporter homes in on only the content words.

Jotters and pencils.

WHAT DID YOU THINK?

WHAT YOU NEED

Notepads, paper, writing materials.

WHAT TO DO

Choose a school event (the school play or a football match, for example) on which various people could comment. Ask the children to think of people they could ask to comment on the event (perhaps staff, parents, or children from another class), and what questions they would want to ask these people.

Ask pairs of children to approach one person from their list (you may wish to allocate people to pairs so as not to swamp the head with requests for a statement!) for a comment and, as they listen to what their interviewee says, to take notes.

Ask the children to write the beginning of their own short news story, consisting of an opening sentence that states what has happened and a sentence that quotes an opinion. Suggest that they could start the second sentence, the opinion, with speech or thought words (*Miss Simpson said...* or *Miss Simpson complained...*).

OBJECTIVE
■ To collect and quote opinions for a news story.

ONE EVENT, TWO VIEWS

WHAT YOU NEED

Photocopiable page 21, newspaper stories.

WHAT TO DO

Ask the children to think of some situations in which different people can have different points of view (for example, someone telling somebody off, someone who thinks their neighbour's hedge is too high, or a child being told they can't have a pet). Ask them to make a note of an event in the first *event* box on the sheet, and of the names of two parties involved underneath. Can the children record the thoughts these two people might have in the thought bubbles?

In the other space on the sheet, ask the children to think of another news story they have read, and to think of possible different points of view taken by the people involved in those events. They should complete the rest of the sheet to show the two points of view, then think of possible sentences quoting what each person might have said that could be incorporated into a news story.

OBJECTIVE
■ To explore the different points of view of one event.

QUOTED OR REPORTED?

WHAT YOU NEED

A news bulletin recorded from the television or radio, playback equipment, newspaper stories, notepads, paper, writing materials, board or flip chart.

WHAT TO DO

Play the children your recorded news bulletin. Ask them to listen and make a note of sentences spoken by people who are interviewed. Once the bulletin has ended, write one of the sentences on the board, as quoted speech, for example *Mr Palmer said, 'I was amazed'*, then explain to the children that this could also be written as reported speech, in which the words are not quoted: *Mr Palmer said he was amazed.* Point out the use of first- and third-person speech respectively in each example. Ask the children to turn some of the quotes from their notes into reported speech.

Looking at some of the news stories from previous activities, ask the children to produce a short paragraph including reported speech from two or three people involved in different events.

OBJECTIVE
■ To understand the difference between quoted and reported speech in a news story.

OBJECTIVE
■ To understand how newspaper headlines are constructed.

WRITE YOUR OWN HEADLINE
WHAT YOU NEED
Photocopiable page 22, newspaper stories, writing materials.

WHAT TO DO
Begin by looking together at a range of news stories, asking the children how they think the stories got their headlines. What connection is there between the headline and the story? Look for examples of puns and word play in headlines.

Having looked at a range of headlines, tell the children that they are going to try to create their own. Look at a copy of photocopiable page 22 together and read the stories in the right-hand column. Explain to the children that they need to think of a headline for each story and write it in the space provided. This should be done individually, but share ideas afterwards so children can hear a range of headlines for the same story.

OBJECTIVE
■ To understand features in the layout of a news story.

STANDFIRST
WHAT YOU NEED
Completed copies of photocopiable page 22, a collection of different kinds of newspaper, paper, writing materials.

WHAT TO DO
A standfirst is normally directly underneath the main headline, and is normally the first piece of text that is read after the headline. It provides more information about the story than the headline. For example, a headline 'Dinosaur Lives!' might have a standfirst such as 'Scientists Thaw Out Giant Lizards', which would be written in larger type than the actual story but smaller than the headline.

From your collection of newspapers, ask the children to look for and cut out standfirsts that they can find. Return to the children's completed copies of photocopiable page 22 from the previous activity and ask them to try writing a standfirst to accompany their headline for each of the stories on the sheet.

OBJECTIVE
■ To understand various ways in which a news item can be covered.

ONE EVENT, TWO STORIES
WHAT YOU NEED
A selection of newspapers (all from the same day), board or flip chart, paper, writing materials.

WHAT TO DO
As a group, look through one of the newspapers and make a list on the board of some of the stories being covered that day. Ask the children, in smaller groups, to look through some other papers from the same day and to collect alternative versions of the same story. As they find them, tell them to group the different versions of each story together. Ask the children to read through each version of the story and to note similarities and differences – are there some facts or quotes that appear in every newspaper's coverage of the story? Where do the stories differ? Has anything been left out by some papers but included by others?

Children could also look at the varying levels of coverage given to stories and the way in which this differs between papers. A local paper will make front page news of a story that never features in a national; a tabloid may highlight news about a soap star that receives no mention in a broadsheet.

First sentence

Choose three news stories and use the grid below to help you note down some key facts about each story. Then try to write an opening sentence for each story that answers each of the key questions.

Who?	What?	When?	Where?	Opening sentence

What did they say?

Look at this scene and think about what each of the people might be saying. Write your ideas in the speech bubbles.

It's a fact

Sort these statements into ones that are facts (things that are known to be true) and ones that are opinions (things people could discuss and disagree with).

Spiders are scary	Chelsea is the best football team	Mount Everest is the world's tallest mountain
Our school is the best one around	Two plus two equals four	PE is more fun than art
A spider has eight legs	It's healthy to clean your teeth	The Earth is a sphere
Bread tastes better when it's toasted	Bread is made from flour	Grass is green

Question generator

Imagine you are going to write a news story. What would you want to find out? Write the title of the story in the middle wheel. Think of some questions you could answer when writing your story, and write these in the cogs. Try to use different words to start each question – the ideas around the page might help you.

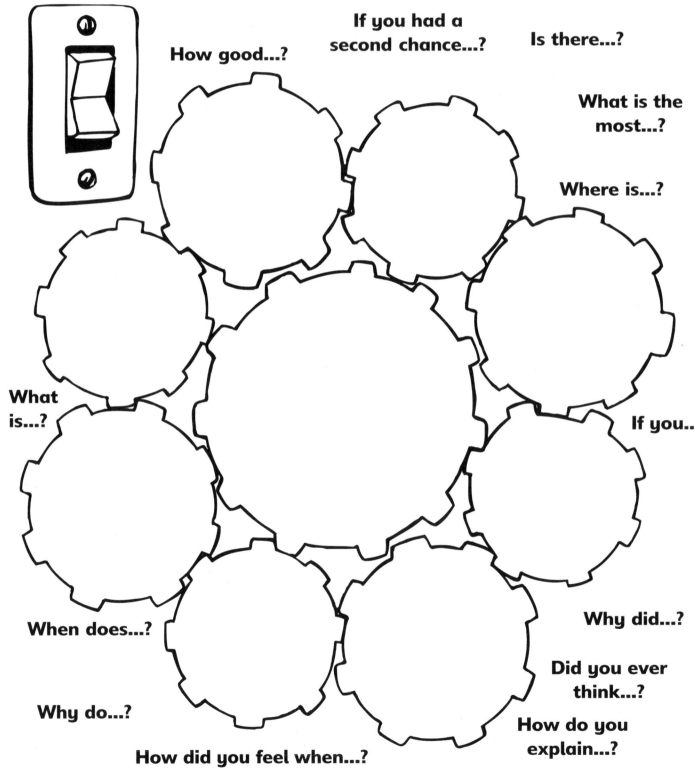

If you had a second chance...?

How good...?

Is there...?

What is the most...?

Where is...?

What is...?

If you...

When does...?

Why did...?

Did you ever think...?

How do you explain...?

Why do...?

How did you feel when...?

One event, two views

Two people can think very different things about the same event.
Use the thought bubbles below to show how two people might have
different thoughts about the same event.

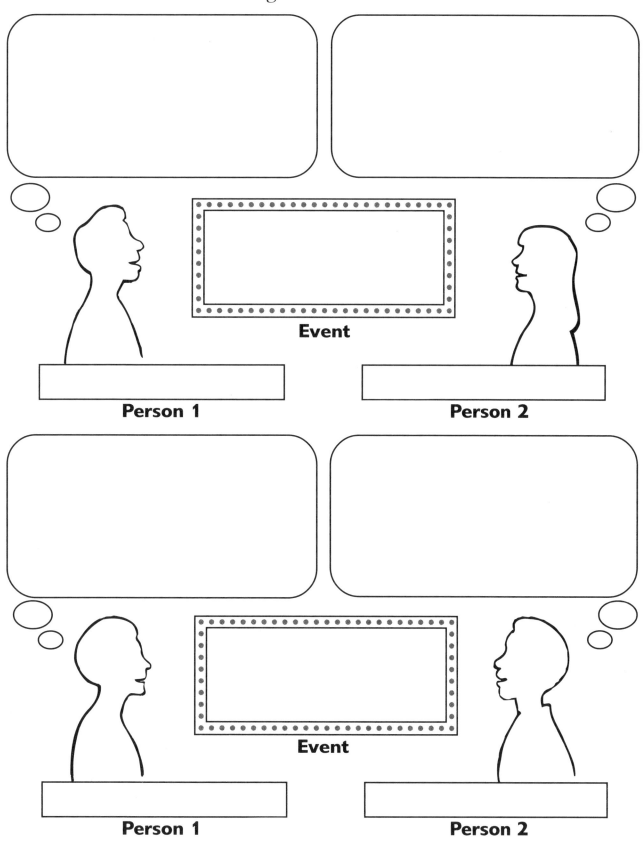

Event

Person 1   **Person 2**

Event

Person 1   **Person 2**

Write your own headline

Try to write a headline for each of these stories.

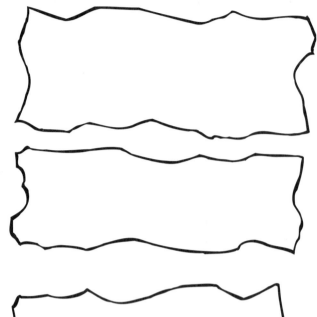

Giant waves have been crashing along the south coast. Freak waves, some topping a massive 10 metres, have caused havoc in seaside resorts.

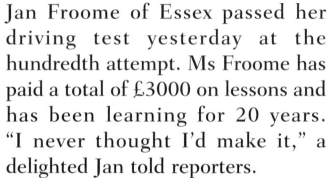

Toodles, the most frightened dog in Britain, is scared of his own tail. The poodle runs yelping if he catches sight of it.

Jan Froome of Essex passed her driving test yesterday at the hundredth attempt. Ms Froome has paid a total of £3000 on lessons and has been learning for 20 years. "I never thought I'd make it," a delighted Jan told reporters.

A baby rhino, Bubbles, has been born at Chessfield Zoo. This is the first rhino born at the zoo.

Children at a London school yesterday arrived to find their teachers were not there. A mix-up had occurred and the teachers were away on a training event. Mum Maureen Fowl commented "It all seemed so quiet we all went home."

A new Christmas card has been invented with a built-in camera that records the words and faces of anyone opening it.

Drawing on the features of a news story discussed in Section Two, these activities guide the children through the process of producing their own news story. Given a set of notes for a story, two scenarios to stimulate writing and templates on which to base their stories, they can build up a page of news.

Throughout this section, bear in mind the following ideas developed in Sections One and Two:

- *why a reader would be interested in the story*
- *the use of headlines*
- *the significance of the story's opening*
- *details the reader will want to know*
- *questions that the story will need to answer*
- *inclusion of quotes and opinions from those involved in the story.*

Burglary!

This open-ended scenario allows children to gather details from which they can later write their report. They need to use the information on photocopiable pages 24 and 25 to piece together and write a report on the story.

Stimulate the writing through role-play activities in which you, or children, take on the part of the police officer, or another eyewitness, and answer questions about the incident. You, as editor, may also like to provide the children with some guidance about the kind of story you want, so they can begin to piece the information together.

They may speculate about the strange robbery, realising that the thieves were frustrated by the closed bank (their intended target), hence turning to the pet shop.

Having made notes, ask the children to write a draft of their stories, drawing on what they learned in Sections One and Two.

News scenarios

Using each of the storyboards on photocopiable pages 26 and 27, the children can write a story about the incident they can see. They will have to consider what they have learned in Sections One and Two, working out what is of interest in the story and what questions their report will need to answer. The spaces along the bottom of the sheet allow them to consider questions they will need to answer in their story as they write up notes for their report.

Before writing their finished reports, the children will need to work out details like the names of the participants, their ages, where they were heading when the incident occurred and so on. They will also need to think of comments from the participants, expressing their thoughts and feelings.

News stories

The photocopiable template on pages 28 and 29 allows the children to develop three aspects of news layout that they will need to consider as they develop their stories: the headline, standfirst and byline. These are marked with different border styles on the page for the children to fill in, either by hand or by using ICT.

The template can be cut into its different features and shared as a group, and encourages children to think about the importance of a story when assigning large or small spaces to stories of different significance – this is a vital process as the children look critically at their material.

Once decisions have been made and stories are written up, children can piece together their front page, using either the template supplied or ICT. They can draw pictures to fit in with the stories, and will need to give the paper a masthead – the publication's title (for example, *The Mirror*) – then photocopy it to give a front page to read 'hot off the press'!

writing guides: **NEWS STORIES**

Burglary!

A burglary has been committed in the High Street, Sheffington. You are a reporter for the *Sheffington Daily News*. Use these materials to compile a story.

From: News Desk / **To:** Ace Reporter / **Sent:** Wednesday 15 February, 13:50

Subject: Robbery at Pet Shop in High St. Sheffington

Two robbers escaped with money and 12 tins of cat food.

Please investigate.

Police statement

At 12.55 today a robbery occurred on High Street, Sheffington. A blue Forxhall car pulled up alongside Shoppo's supermarket on High Street. One woman left the car and entered the pet shop in Sheffington. The suspect reached over the counter and pulled money from the till. The suspect also took a cardboard carton, containing 12 tins of cat food. She then returned to the car and drove south, along Broomspring Lane. The pet shop owner, Mr Alan Gerbil, was injured as he gave chase.

Eyewitness 1: Molly Swan, age 40

I am a solicitor and was on my lunch break at the time. The car came along the road and screeched to a halt outside Shoppo's. I was just walking out of the shop. The man in the car shouted, "I think it's shut, you twit!" and the woman got out of the car and shouted, "We're here now." So she ran over the road. She had long red hair. She went and stopped in front of the bank, then ran into the pet shop. When she came out again she ran over the road and dived into the car. The man shouted, "That was a waste of time! We haven't even got a cat!" and then they drove away really fast down the road.

writing guides: **NEWS STORIES**

Interview with shopkeeper

Q: What happened when the robber entered the shop?

A: She comes running in and stood in that doorway. She looked around and then saw the till. Before I could close it she leaned over really quickly and took the money.

Q: Did anyone try to stop her?

A: There was nobody else in the shop. I moved towards her and she picked up one of the heavy trays of cat food tins. It looked as if she was going to chuck it at me. So I stepped back and off she ran.

Q: Did anything else happen?

A: When she grabbed the cat food a big pile of tins wobbled, then after a bit they fell over.

Q: How did you feel when she entered the shop?

A: I was scared. She looked really wild. I thought, "I didn't go in to pet sales for this."

Q: Did you go after her?

A: I did, but I fell over all the cans of pet food. That was when I twisted my ankle and I couldn't chase the robber.

Eyewitness 2: Hanif Raja, age 28

I was on my way back to work in the supermarket. I had just turned into the High Street and the next thing I knew this woman comes running across the road. It was a long way down the street but it looked like she went and tried the door of the bank, then ran into the pet shop. It looked a bit suspicious so I ran down towards the bank. I got there and tried the door. It was locked. I was about to go into the pet shop and see Mr Gerbil when the door opened and out ran this woman. She had really scary eyes and she threw a tin of cat food at me. It hit my head and I was knocked unconscious.

Questions raised at discussion with editor

■ What did the robbers actually do?

■ Why didn't someone stop them?

■ Why would anyone rob a pet shop?

News scenario 1

Questions

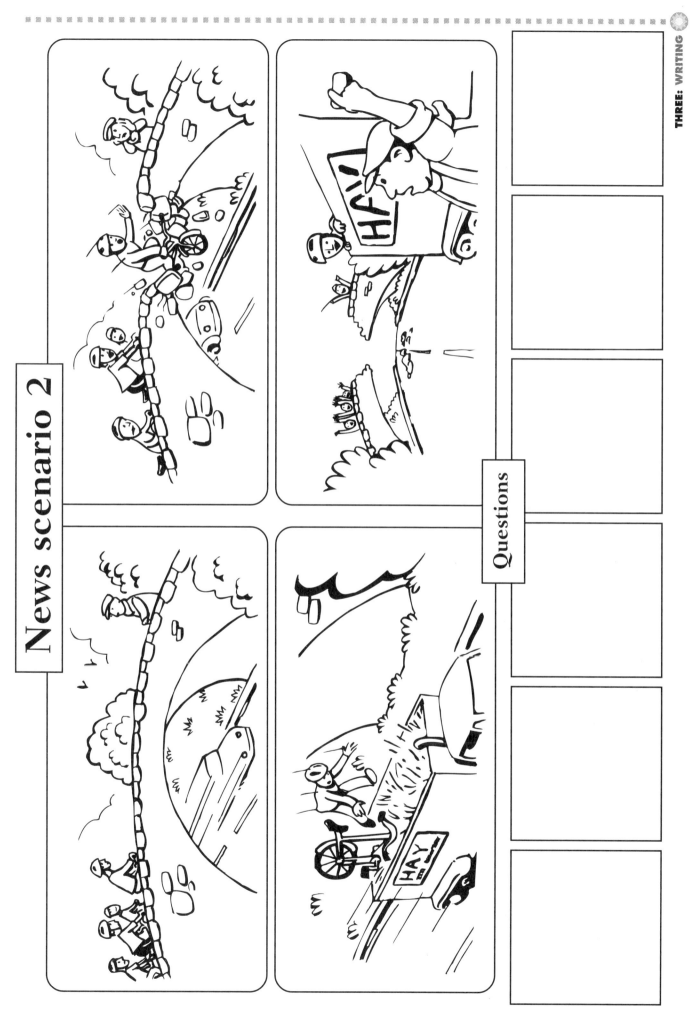

News scenario 2

Questions

News stories

Use this template to make the front page of a newspaper. Design a title for your newspaper and stick it over this space, then fill the other spaces with different features of a news story. You will need to include:

a **headline** that draws attention to the story, for example 'ALLIGATOR ESCAPES'

a **standfirst** with a bit more about the story, such as 'Zoo Loses Dangerous Creature in Town'

a **byline**, with the name of the reporter

a **picture** for one of your stories

another headline for your second story

As part of the publishing process, explain to the children that editing and sub-editing involves vetting work to make sure that it is spelled correctly, that the story is accurate and well-written, and that it fits the space available on the page before it is published in the newspaper. These two activities offer children a chance to reflect on their work.

Review stories

Once they've written their stories, the children need to reflect, and think about how well they have incorporated the features of a news story they looked at in Sections One and Two. They need to consider the interest their story could generate, bearing in mind the purpose of these stories is to sell newspapers.

Photocopiable page 31 provides some questions for the children to consider when reflecting on their work, and will focus their attention on these features of a news story. Encourage them to complete a copy of the page for each story they write, so they can see how their writing is progressing.

Having considered a number of stories, the children could look at refining one in the light of what they have done well in another. If, for example, they used quotes well in one story but another had a better opening sentence, they could combine these elements in improving one of the stories.

Questions answered

A good news story satisfies the reader's curiosity. The shared assessment activity on photocopiable page 32 allows children to swap stories and check that four of the reader's key questions have been covered in the writing. This could either be a shared task, working in pairs to look together at a story, or swapping stories with one another first and then completing the sheet individually. Either way, it allows children to gather feedback about their writing and to note the effectiveness with which the key questions were answered in their story.

Review stories

After you have written a news story, look back at
your work and answer the following questions.

Who will be interested in this story?

What is the most important word in your headline?

What are the three most significant details in the story?

Why did you use one of your quotes?

Questions answered

Ask a friend to read one of your stories,
and to see whether they can tell you:

who is in the story

_____
_____
_____
_____

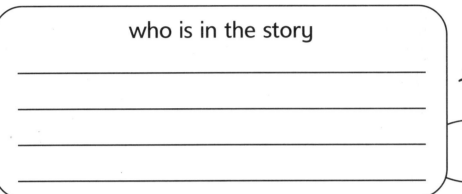

what the story is about

_____
_____
_____

when the story happened

_____
_____
_____

where the events took place

_____
_____
_____

writing guides: **NEWS STORIES**